THE   GIFT

THE GIFT

by
LaBelle Wintheiser

TR
1850
W
C4

THE LITURGICAL PRESS
Collegeville   Minnesota

THE GIFT

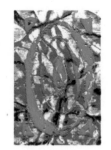

The trouble really started because Haidee was a frisky, young camel who enjoyed teasing and one had to love her as Yala did to put up with her. It was this irritating trick of hers that caused Fazel's jealousy and after that his envy of the turban.

The two boys were rubbing away the dirt and accumulation on Haidee's hind legs, when in a playful mood she nipped the bone fastening on Fazel's shoulder and his tunic fell to the ground. Fazel was so angry that he held tight to Haidee's bridle, to bring a smashing blow down on her nose. With a scream of pain the beast jerked free and this time her long yellow teeth sank into his cheek. Fazel's cries of fear and pain were terrible to hear and he made another attempt to punish the animal, but Yala leaped forward and instead of the beast, received

the blow intended for her. He put his arms around Haidee's long neck and led her apart, crooning in low, loving tones all the time Fazel stood with his hand to his cheek bawling at the top of his voice. Yala, with a final pat of comfort to the animal who touched his face with her thick spongy lips as if to assure him she liked his friendship, brought out the healing tallow and smeared it over Fazel's wound.

A dozen people came running to the spot and Divee, who was Fazel's father, demanded loudly to know the reason for the disturbance. Fazel started to blubber his grief, but suddenly Kaspar's voice silenced him.

"I saw it all," said Kaspar quietly and every eye turned to where he sat in his kingly robes on his black horse. "This boy," pointing to Fazel, "struck the beast in a manner most cruel. I like it not." His flashing eyes turned to Yala and a smile softened his lips.

"What are you called, boy?"

"I am Yala of Melchior's band."

"What work do you do?"

"I am the least of the camel boys and I also help with the goats."

"Well then, Yala of Melchior's band, you shall ride my beast Haidee and care for her and always be ready when a remedy is needed."

"And you, Fazel, son of the head camel man, may take over the work of the goats. And I warn you, treat them kindly lest they hold back their milk." He motioned Divee. "See to it," he said, and galloped back to the head of the caravan.

The hate in the faces of the father and son was terrible to see. Yala looked around at the grinning faces of the others, and he saw that some of them were pleased because Fazel had been taken from his high place in the caravan.

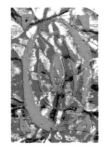

He walked to where Haidee crouched, calmly chewing her cud and stored the tallow jug in its proper place. Haidee nipped at the bone fastening on his shoulder and his tunic fell down, revealing his slim brown body. As he caught it he heard a hoot of laughter, but it was good natured mirth and he grinned back in a friendly way. He flung his arms around Haidee's neck and scolded her in pretended anger. "Stupid one," he crooned musically into her ear, "do not put me to shame before the men. You must learn to leave my cloak alone." Haidee slobbered her big tongue across his face to show how much she loved him.

As he went to his own tent, he felt the scowl-
ing looks of father and son searing through his
cloak and he was suddenly afraid. He flung himself
down on his sleeping mat fighting back the tears.
He had no desire to push himself ahead of Fazel.
Instead he wanted to be friends with him. Before
the caravan moved that night he secreted his precious turban in a packet of pungent healing blos-
soms.

The next morning when they broke camp and
after his own work was done, he went back to the
goats and offered to help Fazel finish milking, but
Fazel cut him off with a scowl and called him a foul
name.

Back in his own tent he fell on his mat and
buried his face in his arms. He was confused and
unhappy and he wished with all his heart that he
had never offered to help clean Haidee the day before, but he liked to see her sleek and beautiful as
such an intelligent and affectionate creature deserved. After a time he went out and got his turban
that was hid in Haidee's load. He brought it into the
dusky tent and held it close to his breast. There was
comfort in the small act, a link between now and the
happy days in his grandmother's house. He forgot
for the moment that Fazel and his father were angry
with him.

Then he heard Fazel in a loud, arrogant voice
calling his name. He began to tremble and tried to
thrust the turban out of sight. But the long, silky
length of linen would not obey his fumbling fingers,

and before he could fold it, Fazel bounced through the tent flap. "Did you not hear me, sneaky one? My father . . . ." He broke off to stare at the turban cloth that seemed even whiter in the gloom of the tent. "Where did you get that?" he demanded and made to snatch it from Yala.

"It is mine," Yala answered, his heart beating furiously.

"You stole it from one of the Wisemen! No camel boy may own such a rich head covering."

"It was my father's, who is dead, and now it is mine," Yala retorted, showing a little spirit and clutching the turban close, "I do not steal."

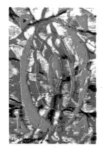

Fazel's eyes glittered as he fingered one end of the lovely fabric. He was only a year older than Yala but he had traveled with other desert caravans since his father was a head camel man, and he was more knowing in all things than Yala. Yala saw the jealousy and cunning in his face. Oh, he wondered, feeling desolate, what more trouble is there to be.

"I shall call my father," Fazel decided, "he will learn who is the owner of this fine turban." He was gone and Yala fell on his mat, the lump in his throat almost choking him.

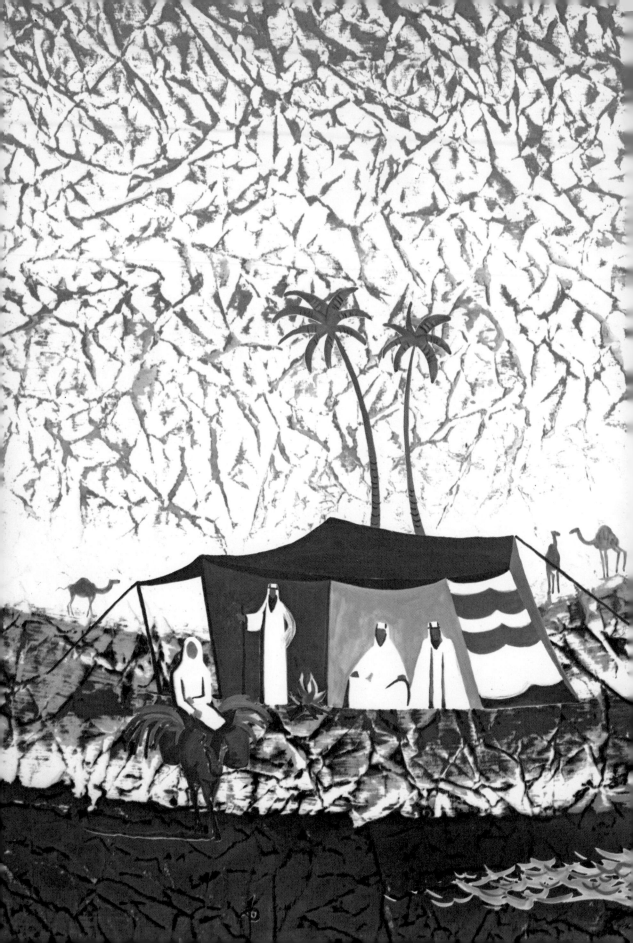

When he joined Melchior's caravan in Damascus, he thought little of the reason for the journey except that Melchior, who was a great scholar as well as a good king, announced that they were to follow a new star that had suddenly appeared in the heavens. It was Yala's first time away from his grandmother's simple home, and the prospect of new places, new friends and possibly adventure thrilled him.

On the fifth night out Melchior's caravan rested by a certain holy well near a bridge that spanned the river Jordan. Here, to Yala's surprise, they were joined by two other caravans whose leaders were following the star.

One was Kaspar, young and hale, riding a splendid black horse. The head man in Kaspar's company was Divee. It was soon arranged that Divee would oversee all the workers in the now mighty assembly. Divee was a tall, lean man, wearing his scarlet turban so that the ends danced over his shoulders when the wind blew. Yala was entranced with this jaunty style and determined to practice it in secret with his own cloth.

The third king was Balthasar, an old man and like the other two a seeker after truth. In his eyes was the same deep vision as in the eyes of Yala's beloved Melchior. Balthasar rode neither horse nor camel but a magnificent elephant whose stately stride led the long cavalcade across the miles of sand.

A dozen goats provided the milk and cheese necessary on a desert crossing. Camels were loaded with tents and sleeping mats, clothing and cushions.

There were enough donkeys to carry food for all and the water bags to be filled when they left the pleasant water spots. When Yala first saw the young camel Haidee, ridden by Fazel, he fell in love with her. She bore a light but important burden, all the healing supplies, soothing herbs, Balm of Gilead, oil from the bitter lemon, sheep's tallow and pungent spices.

Now, in his desolation, alone in the tent, he was remembering all this, and he wished with all his heart he had not offered to help Fazel yesterday morning, but he thought Haidee was so intelligent and affectionate and deserved to be made sleek and shining. He wished he had not taken his precious turban from its hiding place. What could he do if everyone believed the turban was not really his? If Divee declared he was a thief. . .?

He heard their voices and sprang up to face them. "It is such as kings wear," Fazel was shouting and Divee motioned him to silence.

"I will be the judge," Divee said with a crafty look in his eyes. "Give me the head cloth."

Reluctantly Yala obeyed his superior.

Divee snatched the linen and held it up. The fragrance from the sweet dried flowers clung to it and drifted around them; Yala held himself motionless, seeing the malice in the older man's face, fearing him.

"Indeed, a splendid turban cloth," Divee said smoothly, "suitable only for a man and not a youth."

"It was my father's and now it is mine," Yala said respectfully but inwardly cringing as Divee's unwashed fingers defiled the purity of his treasure. "Please return it to me."

"Never!" screamed Fazel. "You are a liar and a thief and I will have it for my own!"

"Not so hasty, my son! I know how to deal with this upstart. . . . I think I will like to have this turban for my own. I shall tell my master . . ."

"What will you tell me, Divee?" The head camel man whirled to stare in confusion at his master who had silently appeared in the entrance. The linen dropped from his hands to the sand floor and both boys lunged to capture it.

"It is mine!" screamed Fazel and jerked it from Yala's grasp.

"Stay," commanded Kaspar, and took the cloth, "I wish to hear all that has gone before." His keen eyes rested briefly on each face. "When I heard Fazel telling you this one had stolen a king's turban I followed. Let me hear the truth. You may speak, Yala of Melchior's band."

"My grandmother wove it when my father was but fifteen. When I joined with Melchoir, she gave it to me, bidding me treasure it until I come into my own manhood."

"When will that be?"

"A year hence. I stand now at fourteen years."

Kaspar studied the linen on his open palms. He nodded to Fazel. "Tell me, Fazel, son of the head camel man, why you claim the turban?"

Fazel shot a look of consternation at his father, opened his mouth, but made no sound. Then he pulled the gray headcloth he wore to cover his face.

"I bought it for my son," Divee said smoothly.

"Tell me where?"

Divee replied, "While we were yet in Persia."

Kaspar studied Divee's crafty face and the rich brocade of his head cloth made a silken whisper in the silence as he slowly shook his head.

"Nay, Divee. This linen was woven on a home loom. I know it well. It is not for sale in city linen marts. The truth, Divee. Does it belong to you?"

And put to it Divee had to confess his lie. And Yala knew, when his turban was restored to him, that father and son were his enemies, hating him more than ever.

Because he was lonely and heartsick, when his work was done, sometimes he crept to the tent shared by the Magi. Unseen, he saw them study their scrolls with the strange markings of the heavens. He heard them speak often of a holy child, whose birth the world waited for. A king, they said, to lead men to freedom and to the one true God. This kind of talk filled him with a longing for wisdom and knowledge and his reverence for them grew.

They were so different and yet so alike in purpose. His beloved Melchior was old and untidy but his was a great and tender wisdom. Beside his mighty beast walked a small camel who had with his burden pieces of gold and an ancient cup of the same precious metal. These, Yala learned, were gifts for the newborn one.

"I will give my lands and palaces," he heard Melchoir say, "so that my children and the children of all men may live under his power and justice."

"And I," declared the youthful Kaspar, flashing his handsome eyes, "will give with the frankincense I offer, all the youth of me not yet lived, all my wealth to follow his banner in sorrow and joy."

The worldly-wise Balthasar, who was more often silent than the others, spoke also, and from his hiding place Yala wondered how could Balthasar possibly meet the generosity of his friends.

He said in a dreamy tone, "We men of Media have believed always that one day we would see the star as foretold in the first writings of the prophets. I follow this star with trust and hope. I will lay at the feet of the one we will find the love of my old heart, the priceless myrrh brought from the distant coast of Coromandal, the proudest boast of my ancient people."

Then it was there stirred in Yala's lonely young heart, the desire to place a gift at the feet of so wondrous a child. He could not ease his mind of the thought by reminding himself that he was unimportant, unknown and so poor that even if there were gift marts on the wide sand of the desert, he had neither gold nor silver pieces to spend in them. But he dreamed of a gift for the holy child so much that Divee cursed him when once he failed to secure properly one corner of a tent and the restless desert wind drifted sand over the sleeping mats, making them uncomfortable.

Night after night the caravan followed the brilliant star that moved with majestic surety across the heavens, until one morning when they made camp, Yala saw they were leaving the desert. In the distance was a rim of hills, whose contours wore the morning haze like a misty veil. He hastened to his secret place and heard the Wisemen say they were coming to the end of the journey.

He thought, "Since I have no gift for the holy One we will find, I will practice wearing my turban so that when I come in to his presence I will carry myself like a man." He did his work carefully so Divee nor Fazel could find no fault in him and when the rest hours came in the heat of the day, instead of sleeping, he took from his woolen pouch the piece of white linen. He let it fall to its full beautiful length and he breathed in the rich sandalwood dust his grandmother had sprinkled in its folds, mingling now with the scent of the aromatic herbs. It felt silky to his roughened fingers and he pressed his face into its pure whiteness. His fingers seemed made of wood as he remembered his grandmother's teachings, as he fitted the turban to his head. Then, pleased with his effort, he tried winding the turban so the two ends fluttered loose as did those of the head camel man.

When he was weary he slept, to be awakened by Divee's harsh voice. "Lazy one," he yelled so all the workers could hear, "was it dreaming of that silly turban you treasure that kept you asleep? I am tired of your sloth . . . ." He struck the boy with the flat of his hand. Burning with shame, Yala hurried to help Fazel milk the goats before loading Haidee.

The sun was going down and above the star glowed with a radiance that dimmed all the wild beauty of the crimson sunset. Yala looked up at the star, as he often did, and thought, "Before I mount Haidee I will bend my turban on my head and wear it all night. In the morning I will hide it again so Divee will not jeer at me. I will do this every night until we come to the end of the journey. Then I will wear it proudly, and no one shall say me nay."

When the time was right, with the linen in his hands he stepped to where Haidee, still kneeling, made a screen between himself and Divee who was directing work some distance ahead. He knelt on the sand and carefully bound the turban, fold on fold, until it rose above his brow like a noble crown, the two ends loose, to dance on his shoulders when the wind blew. He was so intent on his effort he did not notice the camel ahead was moving, until an angry bellow split his ears.

"What now, camel boy? Are we to wait until you put on that silly turban?" Divee was there, his anger searing the boy from head to foot. "How dare you take my headdress for your own?" he roared, "I will teach you to know your place!" He lunged forward but Haidee playfully swung her head between them and as if to help Yala, nipped a fluttering end of the turban and the pile of cloth fell down on the sand at Yala's feet. Suddenly the restless wind had it, and it rolled merrily beyond his reach. He leaped for it, but the wind carried it away, a maddening whirl of whiteness just a hairsbreadth from his fingers. He

made a running jump and felt it in his hand, but the wind tore it away and again it was flying beyond his reach. He might have caught it but a yelp from Divee halted him.

"Stop, camel boy! Come back to your work!" And Yala watched his treasure whirling in gay abandon over the sandy spaces toward the rim of hills until it was nothing but a speck in the distance; then it was gone. He was too stunned to hear the murmurs of sympathy from his fellow workers, too stricken to heed Fazel's malicious laughter.

As Haidee lurched beneath him in the long hours of the night, there was a pain in his young boy's heart, a sense of loss that was almost more than he could bear.

In the morning he saw a great golden dome ris-
ing from behind a mighty wall. "It is Jerusalem," he
heard Divee say importantly, but the name meant
nothing to him. Later he saw the Wisemen, now
dressed in robes of silk, with jewels in their turbans,
ride through the city gates. There was a great tense-
ness in the camp. He did not understand it but all
about were low whispers that revealed that this
visit to Jerusalem was very important. He was burning with curiosity and would not let himself sleep
during the day fearing he would miss the Wisemen's
return. He wanted to learn if possible, the reason
for this break in the journey. He seemed to feel it
had something to do with the baby.

Toward the close of the day he saw them coming
and hastened to his secret place. They all wore a
troubled look and his beloved Melchoir's voice was
very sad.

"I fear we made a mistake to inquire about the child from Herod," he said. "The man has no truth in him."

Kaspar burst out impetuously, "I am the most youthful of us. Yet I saw evil in Herod's eyes when I told him the ancient writings prophesy that one is to come who will rule the world."

Now Balthasar rose up from his cushion, and his friends waited to hear him speak. "Let us consider all things," he said heavily. "Herod is one who has lost his soul. You understand that he is an outsider and only because mighty Rome has use for him is he allowed to rule Jerusalem. He lives in fear that someone will take his throne. He will commit any crime to keep it." Yala held his breath.

"Therefore we must go warily," continued Balthasar. "We will find the child-king and do him

honor. We will wait for guidance from him who placed the star in the heavens. Thus, for a time at least, we will save the child from Herod's evil."

Now Yala's heart was heavy. They were coming to the end of the journey and he had neither a gift for the child nor a fine manly turban to wear in his presence.

The caravan moved slowly each night under the star, through sour marshlands whose reeking breath brought tears to Yala's eyes, past wheat and oat fields shimmering in the silver nights, past little homes dreaming, knowing naught of their passing. They bathed in a shining lake and cooled their throats in springs that trickled from the earth, and in the mornings rested where high rocks made pleasing shadows.

Two more nights and the star led them through the narrow twisting roads of hill country where sheep grazed in the radiance that was like day, and when the second midnight hour was come, Yala felt a difference in the world about him. He looked upward and caught his lip between his teeth. His hands that held lightly the leather ribbon of Haidee's bridle broke out in sweat. The star was making a wide circle in the heavens, moving slowly as if calling attention to itself. It sent out broad stabs of colored light, green and gold and purple that illumined the roofs of a tiny town nestled among the hills. It began to drift earthward, slowly and surely and then it hung suddenly still like a gigantic lamp flaming in the sky.

Suddenly the camp was torn apart with excitement, an explosion of voices, commands to halt, unload, milk the goats, feed the creatures. Yala tingled all over and for a minute forgot he must appear empty handed before the wondrous child.

He hurried to unload Haidee and then his sorrow came again. "Haidee," he whispered, "if I speak to him with my heart, tell him why I bring no gift to honor him. Maybe he will understand. I will tell him how the wind blew away my father's lovely turban." He felt a little comforted when Haidee playfully nipped at his shoulder fastening.

Now the Magi were robing themselves in garments more splendid than those they wore when they visited Herod. In cloaks of kingly purple with gold embroidery on the hems, golden chains on their breasts and wide armlets on their wrists, the emeralds and rubies in their turbans sending forth dazzling fire, Yala thought nowhere in the world could there be such splendid kings as these.

He was startled when Melchior summoned him.
"Carry these," he said kindly and handed Yala a roll
of silk in which were the gold pieces and the ancient
cup. Kaspar carried Balthasar's vial of precious per-
fume as well as his own ivory box of aromatic gum,
whose vapor seeking heaven would be like a prayer.

The aging Balthazar needed the arms of two
camel boys to aid his feeble steps and Yala was happy that he had not been chosen one of them. In a
small way, he thought there was compensation that
he was allowed to carry his master's gift, since he
had nothing of his own.

They set out on foot, passing through the
silent streets of the town. It was very early and Yala
walking behind looked in every direction for the
dome of the palace he thought they would find. After an hour they came to an inn on the far side of the
town. They passed around it and now the star came
down until it hung directly over a cave stable, gild-
ing it with strange and heavenly beauty.

Balthasar took his gift and with the other two, it seemed to Yala, entered the cave with heads bowed in reverence. The two camel boys lay down and went to sleep as any sensible camel boy will do when he has the chance. But Yala could not sleep. He wanted, with a strange urgency that almost hurt, to look on this holy child with his own eyes.

He shook the dust from his coarse brown head-cloth, arranged his tunic neatly and quietly entered the humble shelter. The Magi knelt on the earthen floor, their gifts set out before them. In the background an old man leaned on a staff; then Yala's eyes came around to the mother. There was such sweetness and beauty in her face, Yala felt the soreness in his heart dissolve and he knew he would love her forever. Then his eyes dared seek the baby and his fluttering heart almost leaped out of his body. He closed his eyes, believing he must be dreaming all this. He opened them to look again. He took a step forward and fell down on his knees— for there, wrapped around the holy child, to protect the tender flesh from the rough straw on which he lay, was his own white turban cloth, the linen that had been woven by his grandmother, never to be worn in youthful pride by Yala, but as the swaddling clothes for the One born to be the King of Kings!

KING OF KINGS

They received a message in a drea[m]

so they went back to their own count[ry]

ot to return to Herod,

another route.

Matthew 2:12